CRAZY About CARS

Reflections from Behind the Wheel

Text by **Ken Owen**

Artwork by **David Chapple**

HARVEST HOUSE
PUBLISHERS
EUGENE, OREGON

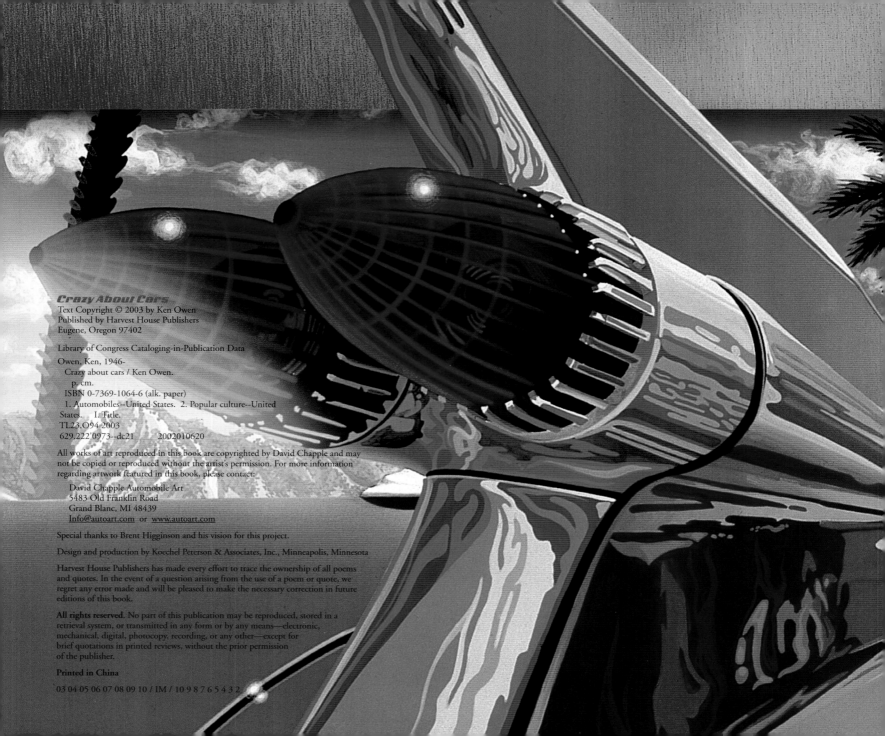

Crazy About Cars
Text Copyright © 2003 by Ken Owen
Published by Harvest House Publishers
Eugene, Oregon 97402

Library of Congress Cataloging-in-Publication Data

Owen, Ken, 1946-
   Crazy about cars / Ken Owen.
      p. cm.
   ISBN 0-7369-1064-6 (alk. paper)
   1. Automobiles--United States. 2. Popular culture--United
States.   I. Title.
TL23.O94 2003
629.222'0973--dc21   2002010620

Special thanks to Brent Higginson and his vision for this project.

Design and production by Koechel Peterson & Associates, Inc., Minneapolis, Minnesota

Harvest House Publishers has made every effort to trace the ownership of all poems
and quotes. In the event of a question arising from the use of a poem or quote, we
regret any error made and will be pleased to make the necessary correction in future
editions of this book.

Printed in China

03 04 05 06 07 08 09 10 / IM / 10 9 8 7 6 5 4 3 2

AT FIRST GLANCE...

The one thing that unites all human beings, regardless of age, gender, religion, economic status, or ethnic background, is that deep down inside, we all believe that we are above-average drivers.

DAVE BARRY

For as long as I can remember, I have been crazy about cars. I am the epitome of a classic car guy. When I was 11, I could name every new vehicle on the road, and throughout my life, cars have played a very important role.

Combine my interest in cars with a passion for ministry, and it is easy to understand why God has graciously allowed me to combine the two. As the president of Christian Motorsports International (the parent ministry for Racers For Christ and Rodders For Christ), I oversee an organization that is committed to bringing inspiration to the world of motorsports as we seek to bring the gospel of Christ to the highways, byways, and speedways of life.

Come along and let's explore why people are so dedicated and fervent in their passion for cars and see what lessons we can learn from behind the wheel. For people who are truly crazy about cars, it's more about passion than practicality. It's more about our base nature to be around these machines than any basic need. That's why we describe ourselves as being *crazy* about cars. And the fact that you are reading this book may be an indication that you can identify to some degree with our peculiar abnormality.

Some have suggested that the popular WWJD bracelets (What Would Jesus Do) may in fact mean: *What Would Jesus Drive.* While I must leave such biblical curiosity to the theologians, I for one still must confess to the existence of certain feelings of a spiritual nature in my loving affection for automobiles—although I'm sure my wife is convinced that it's merely another expression of man's hopeless depravity.

Happy motoring!

Ken Owen

CHAPTER ONE

The First Taste of Freedom

Freedom is the opportunity to make decisions.
Kenneth Hildebrand

Aside from the obvious desire to reach my thirteenth birthday and officially be considered a teenager, the most important objective in my young life was becoming old enough to drive.

I couldn't wait until I was fifteen-and-a-half years old, the age at which a learner's permit was allowed in California. Then, once having completed Driver's Ed in school, the entire focus of my life became walking into the Department of Motor Vehicles on my sixteenth birthday with an enormous smile on my face and a great sense of excitement and anticipation in my heart (a condition that has not been duplicated since, I might add).

Receiving a driver's license is the *bar mitzvah* of western civilization, marking perhaps the first true sense of accomplishment in our journey toward adulthood. Finally being able to drive (without Mom or Dad sitting in the front seat) also leads to one's greatest sense of independence—although fear, apprehension, and unparalleled excitement were all

Your life is the sum result of all the choices you make, both consciously and unconsciously. If you can control the process of choosing, you can take control of all aspects of your life. You can find the freedom that comes from being in charge of yourself.

ROBERT F. BENNETT

quite prevalent during my first solo trip in Dad's '59 Chevy Bel-Air sedan.

Reality finally visited me sometime later, and I began to understand the sense of responsibility and accountability that accompanied each of my motorized treks into adulthood. (My first accident also helped to underscore that reality.) But reality often is preceded by fantasy, and this certainly was the case in my life.

For months prior to my sixteenth birthday, my father would allow me to sit in the car while it was parked in the driveway. His gull-wing '59 became my own personal simulator. As I sat behind the wheel, I embarked on a number of fantasy trips throughout my hometown of Vallejo, California, while never leaving the protection of our driveway (or my father's oversight). I made all of the appropriate stops and turns in my mind and even learned how to properly shift the 3-speed manual trans-

mission. Of course, every shift was silky-smooth—which is one of the many benefits of a fantasy!

I spent hours behind the wheel of that Chevy. By the time I received my license, I had already accumulated untold hours of seat time. And here's the best part. With all of the mental miles I had driven, I never once had to stop for gas or change the oil.

While such independence could easily be considered somewhat risky for those not mature enough to handle the responsibilities (read: irresponsible), driving is one of the ultimate expressions of freedom nonetheless. Suddenly I could go anywhere I wanted, without permission and without anyone even knowing where I was going. Life just doesn't get any more free than this to a young teen! Disregard the fact that, due to my Christian upbringing, most of the solo trips during my early years of driving were to church and to church-related functions. The point was I now had the freedom to be as irresponsible as I wanted to be—even if I didn't have the desire.

I am convinced that this overwhelming sense of freedom and independence at such an early age endears the automobile to us in a most unique way. It is a bonding that lasts a lifetime, explaining (in part) why we are so attached to the vehicles we drive. They continue to be an ongoing reminder of our first taste of freedom. ◆

Travel Log

Did You Know?

• Most states have the minimum age requirement of 16 to obtain a driver's license. You can be 15 in South Carolina and Idaho, but in Idaho you can only drive during the day. New Jersey makes teens wait until they're 17 for that first taste of freedom.

CHAPTER TWO

One of a Kind

Happiness...it lies in the joy of achievement, in the thrill of creative effort.

Franklin Delano Roosevelt

Why do we have such a long-standing love affair with the automobile? In a word—originality. I believe the concept of originality is one of the strongest needs of the human psyche, and for the last century the automobile has provided an ideal platform for true expressions of individuality.

There is an inexplicable rule of thumb among car fanatics that is difficult to explain. I initially became aware of this during my high school years when I began to consider the purchase of my first car (which, incidentally, didn't happen until my second year of college). I began to realize the subtle and unspoken objective was to own a car that was just like every other cool guy's car—only different! In other words, it had to be similar enough to meet certain expectations so that you felt you were accepted—even envied—but you still wanted something that was totally unique to you.

To the true automotive enthusiast, it is important to personalize one's vehicle in a way that satisfies this need to be original and

Did You Know?

- In 1919, a compass and camera were offered as standard equipment on the Templar Touring Roadster.

- The first known car stereo was developed by Earl Muntz according to *Billboard* magazine. It was a 110-volt system that was modified to run off the car battery to avoid the risk of electrocution.

unique. Just as God has created us as unique individuals, so we desire to create individuality in our lives, and the automobile becomes a great outlet for this need to express uniqueness.

It didn't take long for the marketing gurus to catch on. There is an enormous aftermarket industry that caters to this very need. We've come a long way since the days of fuzzy dice, dual antennas, and fender skirts. In today's automotive world, originality is likely to be expressed through 1,000-watt stereo systems, high-dollar custom wheels, and graphic paint jobs. Walk into any auto-parts store and you will be bombarded by displays and advertisements for various accessories and personalized goodies for your vehicle.

When it comes to personalizing a vehicle, however, the most exciting experience is purchasing a brand new car. One of the best things about buying a brand new vehicle is the enjoyment in ordering a car just the way we want it. From the color to the various accessories, we love the freedom to choose and the opportunity to express our creativity and originality by what we drive.

We seem to have a deep need to celebrate our uniqueness. This becomes evident in our desire to "show off" the unique changes and modifications we make to our vehicles. Not only do we want to identify with specific aspects of automotive individuality, but we also want the world to know about it.

I grew up around drag racing in the 60s where cars once raced with such colorful names as the Chi-Town Hustler, the MoTown Missile, Pandemonium, the Bounty Hunter, the Freight Train, and the Swamp Rat. But guys never give names to their personal, everyday vehicles because they're already an expression of uniqueness—no name needed. ◆

The ability to relate and to connect, sometimes in odd and yet striking fashion, lies at the very heart of any creative use of mind, no matter in what field or discipline.

GEORGE J. SEIDEL

We need to give each other space to grow, to be ourselves, to exercise diversity. We need to give each other space so that we may both give and receive such beautiful things as ideas, openness, dignity, joy, healing, and inclusion.

MAX DEPREE

CHAPTER THREE

Purchasing Power

People can have the Model T in any color—
so long as it's black.

Henry Ford

I would imagine for most young people a car is the first major possession of their lives. Regardless of how it comes about—whether purchased with personal funds or given as a gift from Dad—that first vehicle comes with a great sense of pride.

I believe that this pride in ownership provides a significant boost to our maturity. Every young person who enjoys that pride of ownership learns the same important lesson that Adam had to learn in the Garden of Eden—throughout his life, man was to be a good steward of those things placed in his control. He would be responsible and accountable for his possessions.

When I purchased my first car during my sophomore year of college, I was overwhelmed with a sense of pride and satisfaction. That yellow and white '57 Chevy helped me learn a number of lessons about personal responsibility and accountability. In fact, it created a platform for many of the ongoing lessons of adulthood that were to follow.

I treated my first car like my firstborn. I pampered it, nurtured it, protected it, and gave it everything it needed and demanded. While I will admit to a degree of over-indulgence, it taught me some very valuable lessons concerning the importance of proper stewardship and responsibility because it represented the greatest amount of money I had ever expended to that point in my life.

I worked hard for the money required to purchase that car, and I was quite intent on protecting my investment. With ownership came pride. And with pride came a stronger incentive to be responsible.

One of the great epiphanies of my young adult life came when it was time to sell my first car. It happened after I realized for the first time that someone else wanted my car more than I did. And I can still remember quite vividly the sense of power that I felt upon realizing that I was totally free to establish whatever value I considered appropriate.

That inaugural entrepreneurial exercise helped to usher me into the realm of personal commerce like no other experience in my memory. Buying and selling my first car made me realize that I was indeed capable of surviving the challenges of a business-oriented world. I even made it through the bureaucratic maze at

> *Windshields are God's way of allowing us to see His beauty at 65 mph and protect us from bugs in our teeth.*
>
> ROGER SCOTT

> *Growth means change and change involves risk, stepping from the known to the unknown.*
>
> GEORGE SHINN

the Department of Motor Vehicles on my own with relative ease and minimal emotional damage.

The next noble adventure in my automotive journey through life came when I purchased my first *new* car—a 1968 Chevy Nova. This will remain in my memory as one of life's great moments. I was working for a Chevrolet dealership in San Jose, California, while completing my Master's degree at Santa Clara University. Working for a Chevrolet dealership at that point in my life was the closest thing to *heaven on earth* that I could ever experience. Furthermore, not only was I in a position to order a new car for the first time ever, but I actually received an employee discount. Life just doesn't get any better!

Not too many years later I experienced another life-changing ownership lesson. During a time of financial challenge in my life, I faced the possibility of losing the 1970 Chevy Malibu I had recently purchased. While God was gracious to provide for

my needs (as He always does) and I was able to keep the car, I still had to face the option of not having it. That experience taught me an enormous lesson in values and gave me new insight into how strongly we hold on to such superficial possessions.

From that point on, there has been a deep-seated—yet healthy—sense of pride with each automotive acquisition in my life. God has taught me to take pride in the possessions that He enables me to enjoy, and I have sought over the years to adequately maintain the proper balance of satisfaction and gratefulness. ◆

Did You Know?

- Based on a recent survey, safety concerns ranked below conveniently placed cup holders and adequate sound systems when consumers were asked what influenced them in buying a car.

- Windshield wipers were offered as standard equipment beginning in 1923.

CHAPTER FOUR

Artistry on Wheels

Any form of art is a form of power, it has impact, it can effect change—it can not only move us, it makes us move.

Ossie Davis

Have you ever thought about the artistic impact that automobiles have had on our society? They have permeated our culture over the years seeping into the world of art, music, television, and films. These venues helped create and ultimately nurture the truly romantic relationship between people and their vehicles.

MUSIC

The evidence that cars have impacted our music was never more evident than it was during the 60s. Many "Top 40" tunes were written about cars—a Deuce Coupe, a 409, a Little GTO, a Cobra, a Hot Rod Lincoln …and, yes, even a Nash Rambler! Ironically, many of those songs far outlasted the cars they were written for.

CINEMA

For decades our world has been fascinated and captivated by the silver screen, where the automobile has also made its presence known. Cars and hot rods have been the focal point of many films and television programs over the years. Can anyone remember James Dean in *Rebel Without a Cause* and not picture his fabulous '50 Merc? And the black-primered '55 Chevy in *Two Lane Blacktop* has become a cultural icon even to this day in many automotive circles.

TELEVISION

It's virtually impossible for me to drive through the hilly streets of San Francisco without mentally becoming Steve McQueen in his awesome Ford Mustang—the one that seemed to spend more time in the air than on the ground. And it goes without saying that the most famous General in all of automobile history was an orange Dodge Charger from Hazzard County that reigned supreme during a time when Dukes ruled the land.

From *American Graffiti* to *Christine* and *My Mother the Car* to *Car 54, Where Are You?*, automobiles have solidified a significant spot in our culture. And lest you think such automotive mania passed away after the 60s and 70s, along comes the movie *The Fast and the Furious* in the new millennium, thoroughly captivating society's newest assemblage of adolescent gearheads.

As a teenager in the early 60s, there were few priorities in my life with greater importance than sitting in front of the television each week watching *Route 66*. Somehow, in the innocence of my illogical adolescence, two guys traveling across the United States in a two-seat Corvette with a very small trunk appeared to be the ultimate adventure. I vowed then I would one day become the proud owner of a 1961 Corvette convertible—just like the one driven by Buz and Tod.

The aforementioned car of my dreams did not become a permanent resident in the Owen household until my fifty-third birthday, but I still kept the fire fueled for all those years. Disregard the fact that it cost me ten times more than the original car that graced the dreams of young boys everywhere throughout the 60s. And, yes, you're even welcome to count the number of Route 66 signs that now adorn my garage.

FINE ART

Even in the world of art, the automobile has been a focal point of many paintings and sculptures. Walk through any art gallery or museum (or my garage), and you will find numerous expressions of automotive-oriented art, representing everything from the Model T to the Stanley Steamer.

In 1951, New York's Museum of Modern Art had an exhibit that showcased eight automobiles proclaiming that cars were more than just mere conveyances, they were a recognizable form of art—actual rolling sculptures.

Whether they're on the big screen or hanging on a museum wall, cars seem destined to captivate our attention in the future and continue to permeate our culture. ◆

Did You Know?

- In 1973, *American Graffiti* was nominated for five Academy Awards.

- "Little GTO" by Ronnie and the Daytonas peaked on the album charts at number four in 1964.

Making the simple complicated is commonplace; making the complicated simple, awesomely simple, that's creativity.

CHARLES MINGUS

Match the following movie or television program with the vehicle it featured:

1. Smokey and the Bandit
2. Route 66
3. Starsky & Hutch
4. Christine
5. Bullitt
6. Nash Bridges
7. Magnum PI
8. The Fast and the Furious
9. Herbie the Love Bug
10. Any James Bond movie

A. VW Beetle
B. Mitsubishi GT
C. Plymouth Barracuda
D. Pontiac Trans Am
E. Chevrolet Corvette
F. Ford Torino
G. Aston-Martin
H. Ferrari 308
I. Ford Mustang
J. Plymouth Fury

1. D. 2. E3. F4. J5. I6. C7. H8. B9. A 10. G

CHAPTER FIVE

Purpose and Practicality

He has gained every point who has mixed practicality with pleasure.

Horace

Not everyone is crazy about cars for the same reasons. For some, their attachment to the automobile is due to necessity more than any expression of affection. For these people, a vehicle is merely a practical tool of transportation. While some may argue whether these constitute legitimate "car people," they do have a very identifiable relationship with their vehicles.

Ironically, my father fit into this category. While he had a very strong attachment to his vehicles, he related to them almost entirely on the basis of their usefulness. In fact, the more basic, the better! Dad's cars seldom had any accessories, let alone any items even remotely associated with luxury and comfort. As long as Chevrolet continued to sell cars with standard transmissions and 6-cylinder engines, life was good in the Owen household.

The first new car that I can remember us owning was the '59 Bel-Air in which I learned to drive. But while it was a new car when Dad purchased it, it came (by Dad's design) without power steering, power brakes, or much else more than a radio (AM only) and heater.

And of course, the aforementioned 6-cylinder with 3-speed tranny.

To this very day, I can still see the anguish in Dad's eyes when he decided to purchase a 1988 Chevy Caprice for my mom—only to discover that Chevrolet no longer offered a standard transmission or a straight-six engine. Furthermore, by the late-80s, power steering and power brakes were standard equipment. It was almost more than Dad could bear. But, alas, he decided to join the twentieth century, and the look of anguish in his face slowly evolved into smiles of approval over the newly found power and enjoyable convenience.

Such a practical approach to motoring may appear to depreciate any sense of true excitement, but that's part of the universal attractiveness of the automobile. In this case the automobile is the ultimate expression of functionality, as it seeks to be all things to all people. To our utilitarian friends, the primary purpose of the automobile is to go from point A to point B with as much efficiency (and as little fanfare) as possible.

There are many types of vehicles that fall into this category, including those used for work purposes, basic transportation, and delivery services, along with the current crop of SUVs (sport utility vehicles). From soccer moms to plumbers, there is an automobile manufactured to address every imaginable need known to man. ◆

Would that we had spent one whole day well in this world!

THOMAS À KEMPIS

Did You Know?

- In 2001, more than 23 percent of the women who purchased cars opted for the popular sport utility vehicle. Move over, minivans!

- The average age of people who buy Porsches is 43, according to a study by the *Wall Street Journal*.

CHAPTER SIX

A Work in Progress

*The creative mind plays with
the object it loves.*

Carl Jung

There is a popular admonition in the world of machinery and things motorized that states: *"If it isn't broke, don't fix it."* Unfortunately, whoever penned those words did not understand car people. One of the true joys of people who enjoy cars is the opportunity to *tinker* with their vehicles. Ironically, this desire to tinker and fix things has no direct bearing on the need for anything to be fixed! All that tinkering merely fulfills a deep inner desire for people to be mechanically active and emotionally connected to their vehicle.

It's quite fascinating to listen to some car aficionados describe a recent modification or repair. Not only is there a great sense of pride in their accomplishment—no matter how simple or basic—they will often communicate the impression that they have helped or benefited their vehicle in some way. In a strange (albeit mechanical) sense, it seems to address man's basic need to nurture and care.

Many people are inventive, sometimes cleverly so.
But real creativity begins with the drive to work on and on and on.

MARGUERITTE HARMON

God created the need in us for improvement and achievement. Ideally, this need is designed to motivate us to seek continual improvements in ourselves, but often this need is manifested in other areas as well. With car people, this need is expressed by the amount of effort and attention expended on their prized possession.

Some car guys will admit that they derive more enjoyment from the process of a project than from its actual fulfillment. I have known many car people who suddenly became eager to sell their vehicle as soon as it was completed, even after expending enormous amounts of emotion and energy over months, and perhaps years. Once the job is done, they are ready to move on to the next challenge, seeking a new opportunity to put their mechanical and creative skills to optimum use.

The quickest way to recognize these mechanically oriented people is to visit their garage. We're talking tools! Every tool imaginable. There's a tool for every job—even those that may be required only once or twice in a lifetime. The important thing is that every tool is available *if and when* it's

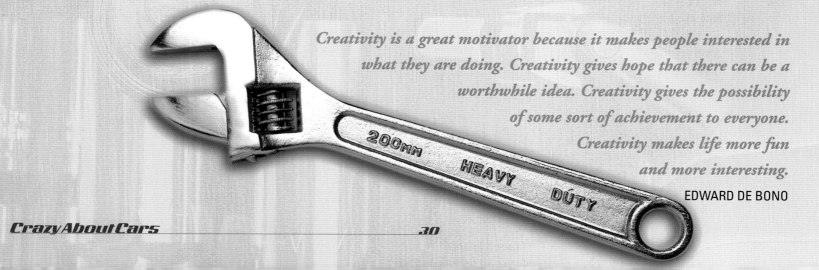

Creativity is a great motivator because it makes people interested in what they are doing. Creativity gives hope that there can be a worthwhile idea. Creativity gives the possibility of some sort of achievement to everyone. Creativity makes life more fun and more interesting.

EDWARD DE BONO

needed. It's the ultimate fulfillment of the Boy Scout admonition to be prepared at all times.

Running water and electricity are desirable luxuries to be sure, but a large tool chest filled with all the right tools provides a measure of satisfaction and security beyond man's ability to adequately explain (and usually beyond a woman's ability to comprehend).

Man's desire to tinker is a fascinating phenomenon. As seen from the Tinker Toys and Erector Sets of childhood years to the Do-It-Yourself section at the local hardware store, there is an innate curiosity in some people to know how things work and to seek ways to improve those items in their possession. For these people, the automobile is one of life's greatest inventions, providing the best of all worlds and opportunities. ◆

Did You Know?

• The Red Cross chose Buicks for their first ambulances in 1915.

• In 2002, a car fanatic snapped up a 2000 Saleen S7 Factory Prototype for a cool $432,000. What a bargain!

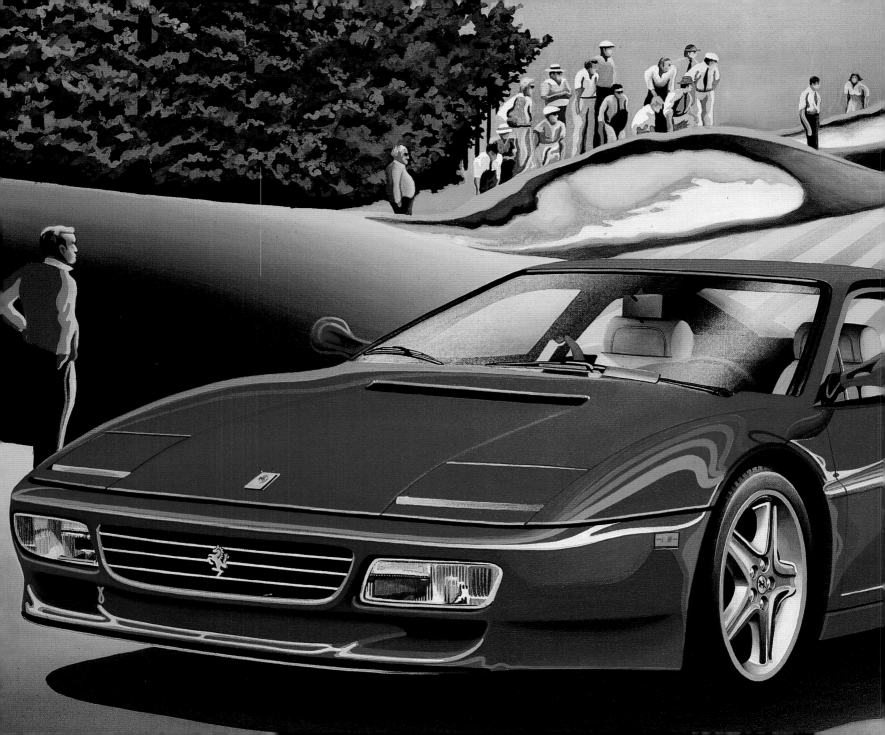

CHAPTER SEVEN

The Need for Speed

Speed is scarcely the noblest virtue of graphic composition, but it has its curious rewards. There is a sense of getting somewhere fast, which satisfies a native American urge.

James Thurber

Almost 20 weekends a year, I find myself in the presence of nitromethane-burning race cars that produce more than 6,500 horsepower each. When one of these exotic racing engines roars to life, race fans will often refer to it as "thunder in the pipes."

For as long as there have been motorcars, there have been manufacturers and owners whose desire has been to create a vehicle that was faster and more powerful than its predecessor. Little has changed over the years.

Hot rodding has always been a part of our car culture and will no doubt remain for years to come. A significant sector of car enthusiasts focus on power and speed. Walk through any sizeable automotive museum or read any book on the history of the automobile, and you will discover that almost every major manufacturer over the past seven decades has had at least one special, high-performance model in its vehicle line.

Car guys like the feeling of power and the sound of thunder that results from the throttle being mashed to the floor—or as the popular saying goes: *Putting the pedal to the metal.* For these people, Thunder Rules!

Assuming you have a sufficient bank account, you can actually purchase road-worthy specialty vehicles from the factory that produce more than 500 horsepower. Those fortunate enough to own such cars definitely love their high-powered vehicles in spite of their expense.

But, traditional hot rodding has never been as much about buying more power as building more power. There is a tremendous automotive after-market industry that feeds the power lusts of these people, offering everything from power-enhancing carburetors and fuel-injection systems to custom exhaust packages.

During the decade of the 1950s, racing and hot rodding came into their own, and it wasn't long before people were seeing high-powered vehicles on the street that a few years earlier could only be found at race tracks or abandoned air strips. Whether home-built in a garage or factory-fresh from Detroit, performance had become a distinctive and accepted part of automotive tradition and Americana.

Today there are actually a few factory-built vehicles capable of going 200 miles per hour in street-legal trim. Over the years, the classic benchmark for a street-driven performance vehicle has always been its 0-60 time—the amount of time required to reach 60 mph from a standing start. During the reign of the factory muscle cars in the 1960s, any 0-60 time less than 10 seconds was considered respectfully fast. Today there are a handful of cars that are actually capable of 0-60 times in less than five seconds. Then again, the aforementioned nitro-burning drag racing cars are capable of reaching speeds of 330 mph in 4.5 seconds from a standing start. Yet these exotic race cars are nothing more than the unlimited evolution of those early hot rods from the 50s and 60s mixed with ample funds and sufficient ingenuity.

While I can totally relate to a craving for more power, I am quite convinced that this desire comes from an inner need that God creates within us so we can relate to the completeness of His infinite power. Whenever I find myself facing one of life's many challenges, my spirit hears God proclaim with supreme confidence…go ahead…bring it on! ◆

Did You Know?

⚙ The first speeding ticket was issued in 1906.

⚙ In 1916, 55 percent of the cars in the world were Model T Fords, a record that has never been beaten.

CHAPTER EIGHT

Ties That Bond

I cannot even imagine where I would be today were it not for that handful of friends who have given me a heart full of joy. Let's face it, friends make life a lot more fun.

Charles R. Swindoll

There is no question that people love cars for a variety of reasons. But people who are truly crazy about cars and who enjoy attending automotive events will tell you one of the most common reasons is: People. For them, cars have become the means by which they are able to relate to other people and develop special friendships. In other words... *people who love cars love people who love cars.*

Car shows and cruise-ins have become very popular and they provide ideal opportunities for people with common interests to come together. These gatherings are as much about people as they are about vehicles. Throughout my years of involvement with automotive events, I have recognized that there is a very special camaraderie among the people who participate in them. An encouraging aspect of this camaraderie is the strong family participation. Cars provide a wonderful opportunity for families to spend quality time together in their pursuit of a shared interest. Many times this bonding takes place among all members of a family, not just between fathers and sons.

Car people truly enjoy the social interaction of spending time together or in someone's garage while

working on cars. Car shows and hot-rodding events also provide an excellent opportunity to sit around and swap stories. To these people, every hot-rodding event is a social function.

Most people who are serious about their cars are involved in some type of car club or group affiliation that is automotive-oriented and most take that affiliation seriously. Guys, for instance, may never debate over their favorite brand of cereal or clothing, but they will quickly debate over their favorite choice of cars. It is not uncommon for car guys to have a strong loyalty to certain tools, yet they will never form "tool clubs" based on their favorite brand. But they will do so for their favorite brand of car.

Car clubs are formed for every imaginable purpose and reason. There are clubs for specific makes of vehicles, such as the Late Great Chevys, the National Mustang Club, or the Mopar Club of America. There are clubs for classic cars, vintage vehicles, trucks, fully customized cars, and import cars—just to name a few. You can even find clubs for cars that are no longer manufactured, such as Studebakers, Edsels, and Hudsons. And while vehicles become the focus and purpose of these clubs, the social relationships and interaction within these groups appear to be a big reason why car owners join them.

You can easily recognize enthusiasts at an early age because they have an intense interest and desire to hang around cars and car people—this would include myself. From parts stores to repair shops, from dealerships to car shows, there is a strong attraction that demands our attention.

When I was young, new car introductions were big events in my life. September soon became my favorite month (in spite of school starting) because that was when most new models were introduced in dealer showrooms—usually under enticing secrecy and mystery. For weeks in advance, the dealers would promote a specific date as the official debut of their new models and it was imperative that I be there on that day. But that wasn't enough. In most cases, my buddies and I would visit the various dealerships the night before, trying to get an early sneak preview through an open spot in the showroom curtains. Of course, that was when new cars actually looked different from the previous models, so those days of excitement are now a fading memory.

My closest friends in high school were people with whom I bonded primarily due to our common love and interest in cars and hot rodding. This common interest created an instant attachment in many cases, and most of those friendships remain to this day. While many of our schoolmates were attending parties and dances and various

*Keep your friendships
in repair.*
RALPH WALDO EMERSON

social functions, we were spending our time at the local A&W drive-in downing root beer floats and discussing tire sizes and carburetors. But at least it kept us out of trouble (except for the occasional impromptu street race down Jefferson Avenue).

For as long as I can remember, I have enjoyed being around cars. And car people. In some circles, people like me would be considered *groupies*. Nonetheless, there has always been an undeniable desire in my life to be around people who are also crazy about cars. ◆

Did You Know?

- NASCAR's Winston Cup series attracts more than 6.3 million people to its 33 events during the year. Nine of the top ten largest sporting events held in this country are motorsport related.

- The first National Automobile Show was held in New York in 1900.

CHAPTER NINE

High-Powered Entertainment

The courage to imagine the otherwise is our greatest resource, adding color and suspense to all our life.
Daniel Boorstin

The term motorsports is very inclusive and incorporates an entertaining milieu of automotive-related events and activities. Studies indicate that as many as 100 million Americans follow motorsports in some form or another, either as participants or spectators. This is a significant portion of our nation's population and helps to explain the growing interest in racing and motorsports.

Motor racing has one of the largest and most popular followings of any sport in recent generations, with sanctioned participation involving every type of motorized competition imaginable. Add to this the many non-racing events that exist today, and it's easy to see why motorsports has become such a strong market in which a growing multitude of companies and businesses are now involved.

Within the world of racing, there is a huge following and support base in which people choose their favorite forms of competition—including stock car racing, drag racing, boat racing, motorcycle racing, sprint car racing, Indy car racing, sports car racing, go-kart racing, snowmobile racing, and even lawn-mower racing. Yes, lawn-mower racing—the ones you sit on and drive. To those who are crazy about cars and racing, it would appear that nothing remains sacred.

In spite of the fast-paced growth of this sport, the appeal of the automobile continues to expand beyond the racetrack. While it is true that it only requires 33 high-powered race cars to attract 400,000 spectators on Memorial Day in Indianapolis, there are also numerous car shows around the country that will draw more than 5,000 cars for public display. Some car shows have actually been known to draw upward of 10,000 vehicles, in addition to the thousands of spectators who attend these events.

Another growing form of automotive entertainment gaining in popularity these days is the hot rod power tour. A power tour is an organized event (maybe a week long) in which literally thousands of hot rodders will travel together across country, perhaps 2,000 miles or farther. Each evening they stop at a predetermined location and host a major car show before moving on to their next destination.

For car guys, the sight of thousands of brightly colored hot rods running single file down a major interstate is marvelously mesmerizing. Spectators will actually camp out at a highway overpass for hours on end waiting to catch a glimpse of this awesome display of automotive excitement as it passes by.

One of the best indications of the entertainment value that the automobile provides today can be seen on the streets of major cities across the nation every Friday and Saturday night. Cruising has been a national pastime for the past 50 years in spite of the various regulations and city ordinances designed to discourage it.

Cruising reached its zenith of popularity during the 60s and 70s on such famous thoroughfares as Van Nuys Boulevard (Van Nuys, CA), Woodward Avenue (Detroit, MI), and Colorado Boulevard (Pasadena, CA). These road ramblings were to hot rodding what Woodstock was to rock-and-roll, chronicling the incredible popularity of modern

An entertainment is something which distracts us or diverts us from the routine of daily life. It makes us for the time being forget our cares and worries; it interrupts our conscious thoughts and habits, rests our nerves and minds, though it may incidentally exhaust our bodies.

SIR HERBERT READ

---

car culture. It was *American Graffiti* at its finest, and it catered to a car-crazy society that refused to grow up. Drivers of all ages aspired to be part of a culture that even to this day seeks to be duplicated on hundreds of street corners nationwide.

In the minds of many folks, however, there is one final example of automotive entertainment that ultimately defines the pinnacle of driving pleasure and enjoyment. It isn't limited to any particular type of vehicle, and age and cost are not factors. Performance specs are totally irrelevant, and there is no predetermined schedule for its occurrence.

It happens every time you—or you and a friend—or you and the family—jump in the car and embark on a journey. It might be a drive along the beach or a trek to visit the grandparents. It might be a well-deserved vacation or a spontaneous trip to the lake. It involves anything you want to do in that moment and becomes your own unique form of automotive entertainment. ◆

Did You Know?

- The first Polo White, 2-seat convertible Corvette, with red interior, was introduced in January 1953 and was entirely hand-built.

- The Cadillac automobile was named in honor of Antoine de la Mothe Cadillac, the founder of Detroit.

CHAPTER TEN

Love at First Sight

In passion, the body and the spirit seek expression outside of self.

John Boorman

Man's relationship with the automobile has always been a fascinating one to say the least, and it is not inaccurate in many cases to describe it as a genuine love affair. The amount of love and affection bestowed upon vehicles is far more than some humans may experience in a lifetime. People who are crazy about cars appear to ride the top of that pinnacle of automotive passion.

The word *relationship* indicates the existence of an emotional connection between two individuals. While that connection is typically associated with human beings, some car owners can relate to a similar link with their vehicles. The basis of any traditional relationship involves mutual nurturing. While it is obvious that these people enjoy expressing love and care for their car, they will argue that their car does in fact nurture them and bring gratification on many levels as well.

Another relationship indicator is the desire to pamper with lavish gifts. Car people definitely meet this criteria. Some are more thoughtful to their cars than their families and friends. In fact, it is not uncommon for them to

reminisce more about their first car than their first girlfriend—and often with far more fondness.

As a result of this unique love affair, nothing less than the best will do. Only the finest waxes and car care products are acceptable. A car cover to protect it from the sun is a must, and only the best engine oil and additives are allowed to permeate its internal parts. Car guys truly care about their cars, an attitude that can form the basis of a long-lasting relationship.

The profound power of nostalgia drives many people to purchase a car similar to one they owned earlier in life. Some buyers will actually expend the time and effort to locate, purchase, and restore the very same vehicle they once owned by tracking its vehicle ID number, which may require years to accomplish. This typifies the deep connection that often takes place between car and owner and fur-

ther underscores the influence of fond memories from the past. Hopefully we all recognize that automobiles cannot give us love, but they can revive very meaningful memories of our past and therefore become a symbolic representation of those former years.

Currently sitting in my garage is a 1970 Chevy Nova SS that is quite similar to the very first new car I ever owned. For years I desired to replace that original ride, and when the occasion finally presented itself to duplicate my first love, I willingly accepted the opportunity. Unlike some people, however, I have not tried to duplicate my original car in every minute detail (color, options, style of wheels, etc.), but I do enjoy the fond memories of yesteryears that it generates whenever I drive it, especially while listening to the original 8-track stereo.

If you talk to people about the affection they have for cars, you will quickly recognize two things. First of all, they can definitely identify with that kind of unique bonding, and secondly, they are not certain how to describe those feelings accurately. People struggle to find the appropriate words that truly communicate the intensity of their emotions.

Love is all about emotion, and cars create a special kind of emotion in the lives of those who own them and care for them. It may be quite difficult to explain at times, but then again, who has ever been able to explain love? ♦

The supreme happiness of life is the conviction that we are loved.

VICTOR HUGO

Did You Know?

♣ At the 2002 Barrett-Jackson Classic Car Auction in Scottsdale, Arizona, a 1956 Ford Thunderbird sold for $109,080. Now that's love!

Through the Years

1. In what year was the Ford Thunderbird first offered as a 4-seater?

2. What was the first year of production for the Chevrolet Corvette?

3. In what year did Chevrolet first offer a V8 engine?

4. The original American muscle car—the Pontiac GTO—appeared in what year?

5. Dual headlights first appeared on American production cars in what year?

6. What was the best-selling passenger car in 1957?

7. What American vehicle was produced in 1981 that came with a brushed-stainless steel body and no paint?

8. In what year were seat belts first offered as standard equipment?

9. What color is a natural rubber tire?

10. What American muscle car was named after a popular cartoon character?

1. 1958 2. 1953 3. 1955 4. 1964 5. 1958 6. Ford 7. Delorean 8. 1966 9. White 10. Plymouth Roadrunner.